# ALIEN ABDUCTION

Anne Rooney

CLASH
by ticktock

Copyright © ticktock Entertainment Ltd 2008

First published in Great Britain in 2008 by ticktock Media Ltd,
2 Orchard Business Centre, North Farm Road, Tunbridge Wells, Kent, TN2 3XF

*ticktock project editor: Ruth Owen*
*ticktock project designer: Sara Greasley*
*ticktock picture researcher: Lizzie Knowles*

**With thanks to series editors Honor Head and Jean Coppendale**

**Thank you to Lorraine Petersen and the members of nasen**

ISBN 978 1 84696 707 8 pbk

Printed in China

Picture credits (t=top; b=bottom; c=centre; l=left; r=right):
Baptism of Christ, c. 1710 (oil on canvas), Gelder, Aert de (1645-1727)/ Fitzwilliam Museum, University of Cambridge,
UK,/ The Bridgeman Art Library: 24. Bettmann/ Corbis: 15c, 21. Columbia/ Everett/ Rex Features: 29b. Corbis/
SuperStock: 6. ImageState: 1, 2, 4-5, 16-17, 19, 20. Jupiter Images: 12-13. Uwe Krejci/ Getty Images: 28b. Charles &
Josette Lenars/ Corbis: 25l. Julian Marshall/ Alamy: 11. Mary Evans Picture Library/ Alamy: 14c. NASA/ ESA/ H. Bond
(STScI) and M. Barstow, University of Leicester: 25r. Dale O'Dell/ Alamy: 7. Shutterstock: OFC, 5b, 8t, 8b, 9 all, 10, 14-
15 background, 18, 20 (lady), 23. Michael Stone/ Alamy: 22c. Darren Winter/ Corbis: 28t. L. Zacharie/ Alamy: 26-27.

Every effort has been made to trace copyright holders, and we apologise in advance for any omissions. We would be
pleased to insert the appropriate acknowledgments in any subsequent edition of this publication.

# CONTENTS

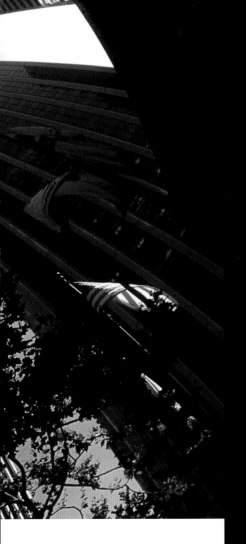

# WATCH OUT, ALIENS ABOUT!

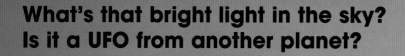

**What's that bright light in the sky?**
**Is it a UFO from another planet?**

Thousands of people say they have seen a UFO.
Many people say they have had contact with aliens.

Some people believe they have
been abducted by aliens.

# Imagine how it feels to be abducted by alien creatures...

## ALIEN ALERT!

A survey in America found up to 1 in 50 people believe they may have been abducted by aliens.

# ABDUCTION

## Imagine...

### ... you wake in the night.

A bright white light is shining in the window. A grey alien with bulging eyes is watching you.

You can't move!

A beam of light carries you out of the window and into the alien's spacecraft.

## You are helpless!

# ON THE SPACECRAFT

**You wake up in a strange room. You are strapped to a table.**

Aliens examine your body. They prod and poke you.

They take some of your blood.

An alien pulls out your eyeball.

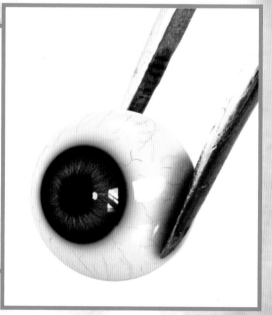

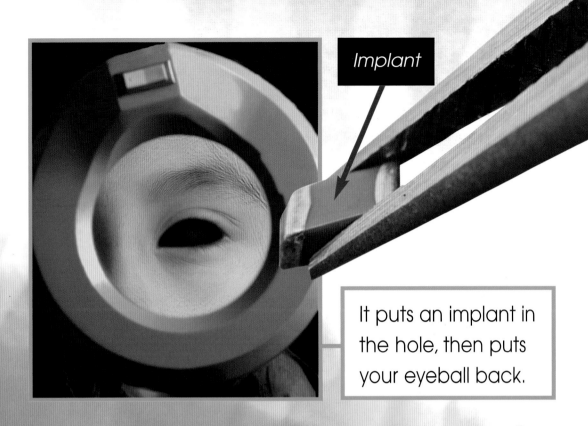

*Implant*

It puts an implant in the hole, then puts your eyeball back.

The aliens show you Earth's future on a screen. The Earth is in danger. The aliens want to warn us. We must take better care of our planet.

# FLASHBACKS

**You wake up in your bed, but you remember nothing.**

You have painful scars and strange burns that you don't remember getting.

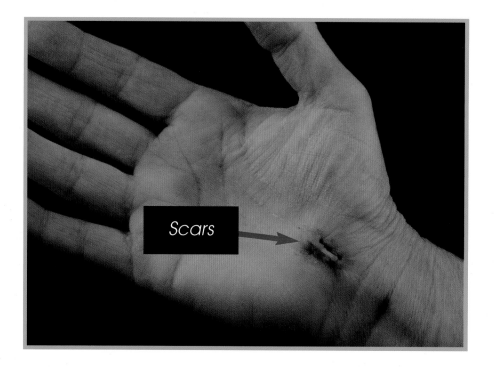

Scars

You feel scared and you feel ill. You have flashbacks during the day and strange dreams at night. Weeks pass, and slowly you remember.

To your horror, you realise you have been abducted by aliens.

You tell other people. Some laugh, but others recognise your story.

You have all been abducted.

# WAITING...

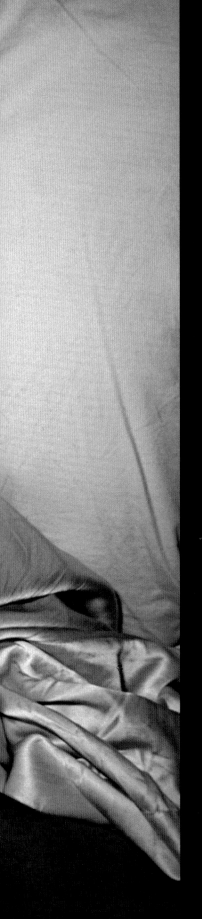

Every night you wait, terrified you might be taken again.

Each morning you look for new marks on your body.

All you can think is – what will they do to me next?

# Will they hurt me again?

It's terrifying to imagine, isn't it?

But many people say this has really happened to them!

# BETTY AND BARNEY HILL

In September 1961, American couple, Betty and Barney Hill were chased by a spaceship.

They tried to escape but were abducted. At first, Betty and Barney didn't remember what had happened. But they had strange marks on their bodies. They had also lost two hours of time.

**Later, Betty had terrifying dreams. She started to remember.**

Betty remembered being taken to a spaceship by short aliens. They had large heads and eyes.

The aliens examined Betty and Barney.

Betty and Barney drew the spaceship. Betty also drew a map the aliens showed her of their home star system.

# ALIEN EYES

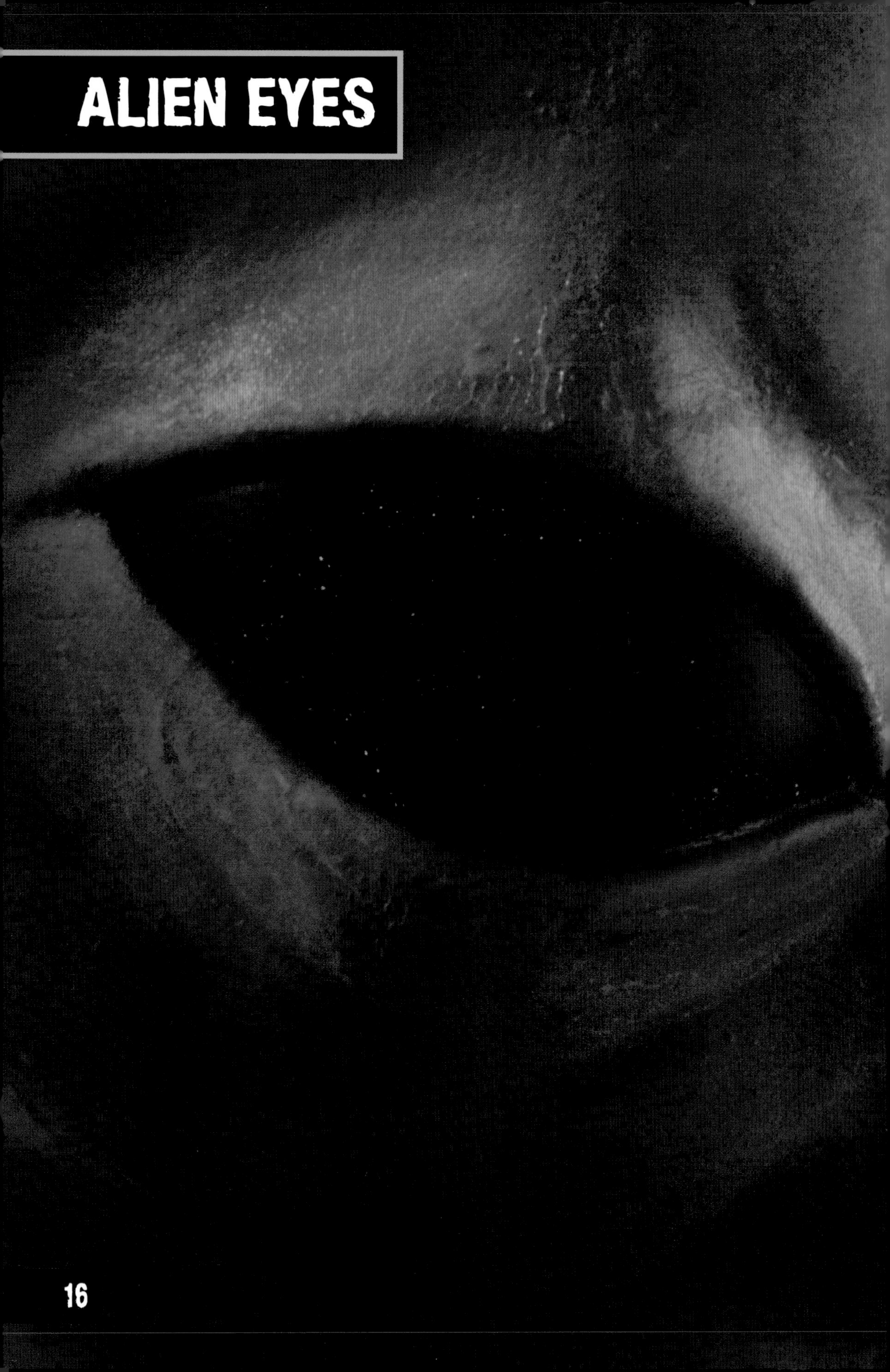

**"I felt like the eyes had pushed into my eyes. All I see are these eyes."**
Abductee, Barney Hill

# TRAVIS WALTON

**One evening in 1975, seven men saw a UFO.**

The men had been working in a forest. As they drove home, they saw a strange light.

One of the men, named Travis Walton, went to investigate.

Travis was paralysed by a beam of light from a UFO. His friends thought he was dead! They drove away.

When the men returned, Travis was gone.

Five days later, Travis turned up in a nearby town. He said he had been abducted and examined by aliens.

# Description of the Travis Walton aliens

Large, bald head

No eyelashes or eyebrows

White, marshmallow-looking skin

Mouths that didn't move

No fingernails

About 1.5 m tall

# FACT OR FICTION?

**Usually no one sees an abduction. This makes it hard to know if it's real.**

Linda Napolitano from New York believed she had been abducted many times.

In 1989, many people saw Linda being abducted.

They watched as she floated from her apartment building towards a spaceship!

**Sometimes abductees draw pictures of aliens.**

The pictures often look the same as pictures drawn by other abductees.

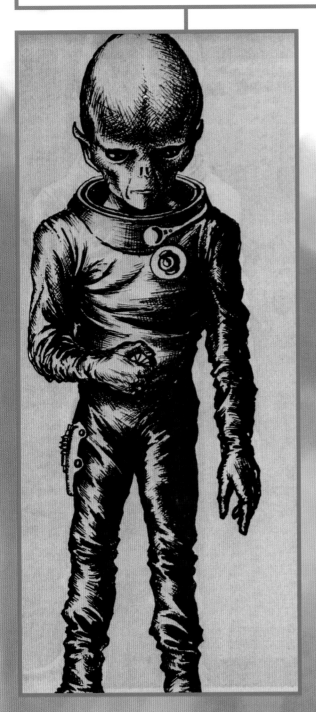

But, the pictures also look like aliens in movies.

**Are these people remembering aliens that they have seen in movies?**

This drawing was made from descriptions given by about 300 people who had seen aliens. All the people remembered the same details.

# ALIENS FROM HISTORY

**Some people think aliens have watched us for thousands of years.**

These cave paintings are from Australia. They are more than 10,000 years old!

**Could these be the faces of aliens?**

In the Nazca Desert in Peru there are giant pictures.
The pictures are known as the Nazca Lines.
Some of the pictures are more than 2,000 years old.
They can only be seen from a plane.

This picture is known as *The Spaceman*.

No one knows for sure why the pictures were made.

Were they made for aliens in spaceships to look at?

This painting was painted in 1710.

The painting is called *Baptism of Christ*. It was painted by a Dutch artist named Aert de Gelder.

**Does it show a beam of light from a UFO?**

The Dogon people live in Mali in West Africa. They tell stories of visitors from the three Sirius stars. The stories have been told for many years. But one of the three stars wasn't discovered by scientists until 1999!

A Dogon ceremony

In the picture above, Sirius A is the big star. Sirius B is the tiny dot, in the bottom left. Sirius C can't be seen. Only radio telescopes can tell that it's there.

**How can the Dogon know about Sirius C?**

**Did aliens tell them about this star long ago?**

# OUR TURN

**There is a story that a UFO crashed in Roswell, New Mexico, USA, in 1947.**

Many people believe that dead alien bodies were found at the crash site.

They believe the bodies were taken to a secret US Air Force base.

This is a model from the UFO Museum at Roswell. It shows how the Roswell aliens may have looked.

In 1995, a video tape was shown to the world.
It showed a dead alien being examined!

The video tape turned out to be fake.

But many people believe the Roswell story is true.
They believe that somewhere there are real alien
bodies. They are hidden in a top secret place
where they are examined by scientists.

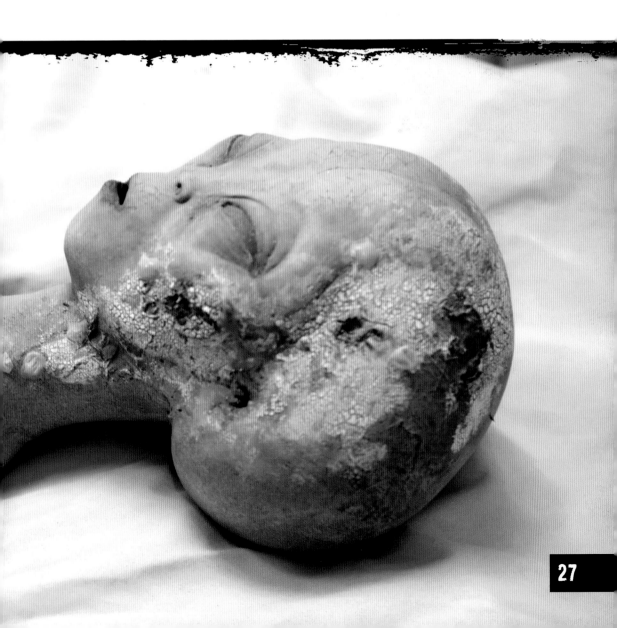

# ALIEN SPOTTER'S GUIDE

Most people who are abducted by aliens say they were taken by Alien Greys. But some people say they have seen other types of aliens.

## Alien Greys

Large eyes

Bald

Grey skin

Up to 1.5 m tall

## Nordic aliens

Blond or white hair

Blue eyes

Pale skin

Very strong

About 2 m tall

**Reptilian aliens**

**Some have claws**

**Scaly skin**

**Long tongue**

**1.5 to 2.5 m tall**

Some people who report seeing aliens say they are visited by men in black. The men in black tell them not to talk about what they saw.

**Men in black**

**Eyes hidden**

**Black suit**

Some people believe the men in black are government agents. Others think the men in black are aliens in disguise.

**abducted** To be kidnapped.

**abductee** A person who has been abducted, or kidnapped.

**alien** A living being who is not from planet Earth.

**fake** Something that is not real.

**flashback** A sudden very clear memory of something that has happened in the past.

**implant** A small piece of equipment put in a person's body by aliens. Some people believe implants send radio signals to aliens. This might help the aliens find the person in the future to abduct them again.

**Nazca Lines** Huge pictures in the Nazca Desert in Peru. The lines of the pictures were made by picking up stones to uncover the ground underneath which is a different colour.

**Nordic** People who come from Northern Europe. They are usually blond.

**paralysed** Unable to move.

**reptilian** A creature that looks like a reptile – for example, it has scaly skin. Snakes and lizards are reptiles.

**scar** A mark left on the skin when a wound heals.

**star system** A small number of stars which go around each other.

**survey** A set of questions to ask people if you want to collect information.

**telescope** A tool for looking at things which are far away. A telescope may pick up light or radio waves.

**UFO** An Unidentified Flying Object. Many people believe that unidentified lights in the sky are alien spacecraft.

# CLOSE ENCOUNTERS

There are five levels of contact with UFOs and aliens.

- **Close encounters of the first kind**
  Seeing a UFO within about 90 metres.

- **Second kind**
  Finding signs of a UFO, such as a crashed spacecraft.

- **Third kind**
  Seeing aliens near a UFO.

- **Fourth kind**
  Being abducted by aliens.

- **Fifth kind**
  Meeting with aliens or making contact with a UFO.

# ALIENS ONLINE

### Websites

*www.bbc.co.uk/science/space/life/aliens/ufos/aliens.shtml*
An interactive map showing famous UFO sightings

*http://www.ufoevidence.org/photographs/view/featuredphotos.htm*
This website has hundreds of  photographs of UFOs

*http://www.roswellufomuseum.com/incident.htm*
A report on the Roswell crash from the UFO museum at Roswell

# INDEX